UNDerStanDIng Sam and ASperger SYNDrome

Story by:

Clarabelle van Niekerk & Liezl Venter, MA CCC-SLP

Pictures by:

Clarabelle van Niekerk

Skeezel Press

Dear Parents:

You probably know or have known a child with Asperger's syndrome. *Understanding Sam* will help you understand Asperger's syndrome and thereby recognize that such children are heroes.

Tony Attwood, Ph.D., author,
The Complete Guide to Asperger's Syndrome

Skeezel Press
2624 Lakeside Drive, Erie, PA 16511 USA

Text copyright Clarabelle van Niekerk and Liezl Venter 2006
Illustrations copyright Clarabelle van Niekerk 2006
All rights reserved

Publisher's Cataloging-in-Publication
Niekerk, Clarabelle van.
  Understanding Sam and Asperger syndrome / story by
Clarabelle van Niekerk & Liezl Venter; pictures by
Clarabelle van Niekerk.
    p. cm.
  SUMMARY: A young boy named Sam, has difficulty at
school and seems moody at home. When Sam is diagnosed
with a form of autism called Asperger syndrome, his
family and teachers understand him better and learn how
to help him succeed. Includes tips for parents, teachers
and children on being with children who have Asperger's.
  Audience: Ages 4-8.
  LCCN 2007939834
  ISBN-13: 978-0-9747217-1-2
  ISBN-10: 0-9747217-1-9
  1. Asperger's syndrome--Juvenile literature.
[1. Asperger's syndrome. 2. Autism.] 1. Venter, Liezl.
II. Title.
RC553.A88N54 2008   616.85'8832   QBI07-600292

ISBN: 978-0-9747217-1-2
Printed in China   Set in PrioriSan and Submarine

Book design by Tungsten Creative Group
Illustrations photographed by Rob Ruby Photography

In memory of:

Willem "Oupa" Venter

With heartfelt thanks to:

Alistair Hartley for your big heart,
consistent support and dedication;
Patty and Ron Merski for always believing in
Sam and being there every step of the way;
to Jody Farrell and Ann Sluga for the fairy dust
that turned this project into such a magical
book; and a big thank you to Mac and
all the kids we work with, for bringing such
JOY into the world.

Love,
Clarabelle & Liezl

UNDERSTANDING
Sam and
ASperger SYNDROME

Story by:

Clarabelle van Niekerk & Liezl Venter, MA CCC-SLP

Pictures by:

Clarabelle van Niekerk

Skeezel Press

Up on the hill where the apple trees grow is a house with a red door. This is the house where Sam lived with his Mom and Dad, his big sister, Emma, and his little dog, Oscar. Oscar was Sam's best friend. He followed Sam everywhere.

Sam loved to giggle.

He would close his eyes, throw back his head, and just giggle. This would make everyone else giggle.

Sam was a happy boy but he was a little different. He did not like loud noises.

He did not like to rough and tumble with other boys.

Making friends was hard for Sam.

Every Saturday morning

Mom made pancakes,

Sam and Emma's favorite breakfast.

Emma liked her pancakes stacked.

Sam did not like his pancakes

to touch.

After breakfast

Sam loved to play his big, brown cello.
He closed his eyes and played until the music
filled up his heart. Oscar loved to listen.

Sam played the same song over
and over again.

Sometimes this annoyed Emma.

On Monday morning

it was time to go to school. Mom said,
"It's cold outside, let's put on your new coat."
Sam started to cry, "I don't like my new coat.
It feels funny."

Mom smiled, "Sam, it's a new coat, what do
you mean it feels funny?" "It hurts my skin.
I don't like it!" Sam threw the new coat on
the floor. He cried even more.

Mom frowned, "Sam, you are going to be late
for school. Let's put on your old coat."

At School, Sam loved to build puzzles. He could build a puzzle faster than any other kid in the class. While he built the puzzle, Sam hummed the tune that he played on his cello.

The other kids in the class did not like the humming. One of the boys said, "Hey Sam, quit that humming." Sam kept building his  puzzle and humming the song. The kids got annoyed with Sam. They decided to play a trick on him. They took one of the puzzle pieces away. Sam could not finish his puzzle and started to cry. They laughed and said, "Sam is a baby, Sam is a baby!"

This hurt Sam's feelings. He cried even louder.

The teacher was not happy. She said, "In this class, we do not bully! There will be no recess today."

The teacher tried to comfort Sam but nothing helped. She called Sam's mom to take him home.

Sam could not stop crying.

The principal asked
Emma to sit with Sam while
they waited for Mom.
Emma put her arm around him.

School
was hard for
Sam.

That weekend the fair was in town. Everyone was excited to go on all the rides. Emma loved the roller coaster because it went up and down. Sam loved the Ferris wheel because it went round in a circle. He went on the Ferris wheel with his dad and giggled as it went round and round.

Sam wanted to go again and again and again.

That night Sam could not sleep. He watched the faraway lights of the Ferris wheel through the window of his bedroom. He put on his slippers and went outside. Oscar followed closely behind.

Sam and Oscar walked and walked...

all the way to the fair.

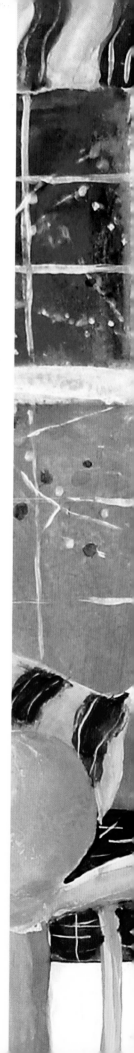

When they got to the Ferris wheel,

Sam sat down on one of the seats. The Ferris wheel started to move. Sam got really scared because he was alone. He started to cry. A policeman heard Sam crying. He saw that Sam was all alone.

The policeman stopped the ride and asked, "What is your name little guy?" Sam was too upset to talk. He just cried and cried.

"Where are your parents?" asked the policeman. Sam could not stop crying.

At home, Dad went to check on Sam. Sam was not in his bed! Mom, Dad and Emma looked all over but they could not find him anywhere. Emma said, "Sam loved the Ferris wheel – maybe he went back to the fair!"

"Good thinking, Emma!" said Dad.

Dad drove to the fair.

That is exactly where he found Sam and Oscar, with the policeman. Sam was so happy to see him that he stopped crying.

"Dad, I went on the ride all by myself."
Dad hugged Sam and said, "Sam, we were very worried. It is very dangerous for you to leave the house alone!"

"But I love the Ferris wheel, Dad."

Dad frowned and said, "Sam, listen to me. Promise me that you will never leave the house alone again." Sam looked down, "But Dad." Dad insisted, "Sam, look at me, never again."

"OK Dad, I promise."

Mom and Dad were
worried that Sam left the house
alone. They were afraid he might
do it again.

On Monday, Sam did not want to
go to school and started to cry.

It was time to visit the doctor.

Doctor Hartley did all kinds of tests with Sam. The next day, they had a meeting. Doctor Hartley said, "Sam has a form of autism called Asperger Syndrome." Mom frowned, "Asperger Syndrome? What does that mean?"

Doctor Hartley explained, "Kids with Asperger's think and feel differently than other kids. Making friends can be tough. Some kids may find it hard to listen or may not look at you when you talk. They may be good at math, or play a musical instrument very well. Others may have an awesome memory but forget to put on a coat when it is cold outside. Working together to understand Sam will help make life easier for him and everyone else."

Mom asked, "What can we do
for Sam?" Doctor Hartley smiled and said,
"It is really important that we work together.
I would like one of my therapists to work
with Sam at his school. She will help him
understand his lessons. She will also help him
with talking and playing with the other children.

"I will write a letter to Sam's teacher, so she
can help too.

"It is very important that we all work as a team."

DUring the next few months,

everyone worked together to help Sam. Everybody started to understand him better.

Things got much easier.

It was time for the school concert. The music teacher wanted Sam to play a cello solo. Sam was very excited. He practiced the song at school and at home, over and over again.

Sam was ready!

On the night of the concert,

the whole town came to see the show. All the kids took turns performing. The choir sang like angels. The ballerinas twirled like butterflies. Even the school band played in tune!

Finally, it was Sam's turn. He wore a white shirt, black pants and a little bow tie. His hair was combed and gelled very neatly to the side. Sam sat down with his cello and held the bow up in the air.

Everyone was very quiet. Sam slowly moved the bow down onto the string. The sound was sweet and soft. Sam closed his eyes. He felt how the music filled his heart. The sounds grew louder and filled everyone's hearts.

He played like he never played before.

WHEN Sam played

the last note, everyone jumped up and started to clap. Sam started to giggle. First just a little giggle, then he threw back his head and giggled some more.

The audience started to giggle, too. And soon everyone was giggling!

It was the best school concert ever!

Mom, Dad, and Emma

came over to hug Sam. Emma said,

"You are the best, Sam!"

Mom and Dad gave him a big kiss.

That night,

Sam fell asleep with a giggle,

a big smile, and a sweet song

in his heart.

Hi Kids, You have just read a story about a boy with Asperger's and how being different is not always easy. You may know someone, or have a friend or classmate who has Asperger's. The most important thing to remember is that we are ALL different and we need to respect each other because of this.

Differences can be things that we are really good at like playing the piano, running fast, or having a great memory. Differences can also be things that we find really difficult like math tests, making friends easily, or doing our chores at home!

The key is to work together because working as a team will help us understand each other better!

Remember that being different is OK.

Keep your heart OPEN.

YOU can make a great friend by being a great friend!

Thanks for being a super team player!
Ms. Liezl Venter, MA CCC-SLP
Speech Language Pathologist

P.S. Special note for parents and teachers. There is quite a lot of information in my 10 tips but I wanted to include the essentials to make it as helpful as possible for you. It may be a good idea to break it down when reviewing with your child or students and go over 1-2 tips at a time, especially for the little ones.

10 Helpful Tips, Especially for You

1. Treat your friend as a regular kid

Your friend wants to be treated as a 'regular kid' just like you. He may want to talk to you and be included in your games so a little extra effort from your side will help a lot.

- Ask your friend about something he is interested in, or
- Give your friend a choice in what game you will be playing, "Johnny, do you want to make a puzzle or play with the ball?"

2. Take turns

Taking turns may be difficult for your friend and playing games or 'talk time' is a great way to help him practice with taking turns.

- 'Talk time' gives everyone a turn to talk, "It is Johnny's turn to talk; Johnny, what is your favorite food?"
- Teachers, you can help with ideas and lots of class practice with your students taking turns. Remember to keep it simple.

3. Change is hard, hang in there

Sometimes your friend may get frustrated or upset if things change; he feels and experiences the world in a different way. He may get really upset and start shouting or screaming – this is not your fault – hang in there.

- For example: If you and your friend play on the computer every lunchtime but one day you decide to kick a ball instead, this may upset your friend. This is not your fault – you can tell your friend it is OK – you can play on the computer tomorrow.

4. Let's keep it calm

Your friend may be extra sensitive to loud noises or shouting. When you talk to your friend, speak in a calm and normal voice. Loud noises can be overwhelming to everyone but especially to a kid with Asperger's.

5. Look at me

One of the things that makes your friend different is that he may find it difficult to look at you (grown-ups call this making eye contact). This does not mean that he is not interested in you or what you have to say.

- It may be helpful to say your friend's name as a way to get his attention and eye contact before you talk to him, "Hi Johnny, look at me … let's go outside."

6. Listen to me

Your friend may find it hard to listen and pay attention so keep your sentences short. This will make listening easier for your friend.

- 'Talk time' is a great way to practice short sentences, "Johnny, what is your favorite book?"

7. Tap for attention

Your friend may be extra sensitive about being touched but sometimes a tap on the shoulder or forearm to get your friend's attention can help (grown-ups call this using tactile cues).

- Before touching your friend, ask your teacher if this is OK. If it is OK and your friend is not listening to you, give a gentle tap on the shoulder or forearm to get his attention.

- Teachers, the use of tactile cues may be helpful for attention during lessons – tap on shoulder or forearm... "Johnny, please get your math book."

8. Let's get back on track

Sometimes your friend may talk about the same thing over and over again. Your friend may not know that he is doing this.

- If this happens, the best way to help is by getting his attention and reminding him of what the class is doing, "Johnny, we are not talking about that, we are talking about what we did over the weekend."

9. Some days can be tough

Sometimes your friend may do things that annoy you. He is not trying to hurt your feelings. Your friend may just be having a bad day and may be unable to 'snap out of it.'

- If this happens, ask your friend to stop or ask your teacher for help.

10. Talking takes practice

Sometimes talking to your friend may not be easy. Your friend may be learning how to 'use his words.' This is hard work and takes a lot of practice!

- You could start talking first. Say hello and ask him a simple question, "Hi Johnny, can you tell me one thing you did over the weekend?"

- Try not to answer questions for your friend. Be helpful by waiting and giving your friend time to talk. If you have waited and your friend is still not talking, you can help by getting his attention and asking the same question again.

- For more ideas on how to start talking to your friend, ask your teacher.